AWESOME DOGS

POODLES

by Breanna Berry

BLASTOFF!
2
READERS

BELLWETHER MEDIA • MINNEAPOLIS, MN

Note to Librarians, Teachers, and Parents:

Blastoff! Readers are carefully developed by literacy experts and combine standards-based content with developmentally appropriate text.

Level 1 provides the most support through repetition of high-frequency words, light text, predictable sentence patterns, and strong visual support.

Level 2 offers early readers a bit more challenge through varied simple sentences, increased text load, and less repetition of high-frequency words.

Level 3 advances early-fluent readers toward fluency through increased text and concept load, less reliance on visuals, longer sentences, and more literary language.

Level 4 builds reading stamina by providing more text per page, increased use of punctuation, greater variation in sentence patterns, and increasingly challenging vocabulary.

Level 5 encourages children to move from "learning to read" to "reading to learn" by providing even more text, varied writing styles, and less familiar topics.

Whichever book is right for your reader, Blastoff! Readers are the perfect books to build confidence and encourage a love of reading that will last a lifetime!

This edition first published in 2016 by Bellwether Media, Inc.

No part of this publication may be reproduced in whole or in part without written permission of the publisher. For information regarding permission, write to Bellwether Media, Inc., Attention: Permissions Department, 5357 Penn Avenue South, Minneapolis, MN 55419.

Library of Congress Cataloging-in-Publication Data

Berry, Breanna.
  Poodles / by Breanna Berry.
    pages cm. – (Blastoff! Readers. Awesome Dogs)
  Summary: "Relevant images match informative text in this introduction to poodles. Intended for students in kindergarten through third grade"– Provided by publisher.
  Audience: Ages 5-8
  Audience: K to grade 3
  Includes bibliographical references and index.
ISBN 978-1-62617-243-2 (hardcover: alk. paper)
  1. Poodles–Juvenile literature. I. Title.
  SF429.P85B47 2016
  636.72'8–dc23
                            2015002033

Printed in the United States of America, North Mankato, MN.

Table of Contents

Poodles are a classy **breed** of dog. They are known for their fancy hair.

Poodle Profile

long nose

long ears

curly coat

Life Span: 10 to 15 years

Trainability:

1 2 3 4 5 6

Hardest to train   Easiest to train

This hair may be fluffy or shaved. It is usually just one color, such as white or black.

Most poodles have curly **coats**.

However, some have cords.
These ropelike twists look
like dreadlocks.

cords

↙

Poodles come in three sizes. The largest are standard poodles and the smallest are toy poodles.

Poodle Sizes

toy miniature standard

Miniature poodles are the middle size.

The **American Kennel Club** puts the breed in two of its groups.

Standard and miniature poodles belong to the **Non-Sporting Group**. Toy poodles are in the **Toy Group**.

History of Poodles

Poodles first lived in Europe.

England

Germany

France

N
W • E
S

In Germany and France, they helped hunters fetch birds from water. Some dug up **truffles** in England.

Some poodles joined the circus.

They were easy to train and performed tricks well.

15

Later on, rich people took poodles for pets.

The dogs are still favorite **companions** today.

A Perfect Pet and More!

Families love poodles for their friendly nature.

People with **allergies** like that poodles do not **shed** a lot.

Some poodles work as **service dogs** to help people with special needs.

Others are **show dogs** or run around courses with tunnels and jumps. Poodles are a winning breed!

Glossary

allergies—bad reactions of the body to things eaten, touched, or breathed

American Kennel Club—an organization that keeps track of dog breeds in the United States

breed—a type of dog

coats—the hair or fur covering some animals

companions—close friends who spend a lot of time together

Non-Sporting Group—a group of dog breeds that do not usually hunt or work

service dogs—dogs trained to help people with special needs perform daily tasks

shed—to lose hair or fur

show dogs—dogs that are the best examples of their breeds; show dogs are judged on their looks.

Toy Group—a group of the smallest dog breeds

truffles—underground mushrooms

To Learn More

AT THE LIBRARY
Bodden, Valerie. *Poodles*. Mankato, Minn.: Creative Education, 2014.

Shores, Erika L. *All About Poodles*. North Mankato, Minn.: Capstone Press, 2013.

Trumbauer, Lisa. *Poodles*. Mankato, Minn.: Capstone Press, 2006.

ON THE WEB
Learning more about poodles is as easy as 1, 2, 3.

1. Go to www.factsurfer.com.

2. Enter "poodles" into the search box.

3. Click the "Surf" button and you will see a list of related web sites.

With factsurfer.com, finding more information is just a click away.

Index

The images in this book are reproduced through the courtesy of: Tatiana Gass, front cover; Jagodka, pp. 4, 9 (center, right); tsik, pp. 5, 11; Teemu Tretjakov, p. 6; Eric Isselee, p. 7; Gerard Lacz/ Age Fotostock, pp. 8-9; GlobalP, p. 9 (left); Juniors Bildarchiv/ Age Fotostock, p. 10; cynoclub, p. 12; Dale Spartas/ Corbis, p. 13; Splash News/ Corbis, p. 14; sergspb, p. 15; GraphicaArtis/ Corbis, p. 16; Edith Held/ Corbis, p. 17; sonya etchison, p. 18; ArtMarie, p. 19; Disability Images/ Alamy, p. 20; Dempster Dogs/ Alamy, p. 21.